EASY EXERCISES
to
RELIEVE STRESS

EASY EXERCISES

—— *to* ——

RELIEVE STRESS

H. Eshref

Photographs by Anthea Sieveking

Adams Media Corporation
Holbrook, Massachusetts

This edition published by Adams Media Corporation,
260 Center Street, Holbrook, MA 02343 by
arrangement with Frances Lincoln Limited.

CIP information available upon request to the
publisher.

ISBN: 1-58062-128-7

Set in Berkeley Old Style by Frances Lincoln Limited
Printed in Singapore

9 8 7 6 5 4 3 2 1

Author's acknowledgments
I would like to thank Helen Morton, Aydin, Yasmin,
Danyal, and the rest of my family for the support
they've given me, and everyone at the BCNO.

Publishers' acknowledgments
The Publishers would like to thank
Nicci Baker, David Batchelor, Nicci Blatchford, Hannah
Jane Bryant, Nicky Ellis, Francesca Illiffe, Alys Kihl,
Ryan Ludlam, Stephen Millys, Ruth Moss, Sara Perkins,
Tom Stewart, Suzanne Swan, Pekoe Tang and Tom
Windross for modelling the exercises in this book.

CONTENTS

INTRODUCTION

There is nothing wrong with stress in moderation. Stresses can be simply those challenges that make life interesting, and tension is a normal physiological reaction initiated by the body to make you ready to achieve certain goals. Life without any stress would be boring. However, when stress is excessive or prolonged it causes problems.

I take a holistic view—that the body affects the mind and the mind the body. Therefore, dealing with the physical effects of stress will relieve the emotional strains, and you can learn to control your physical reactions to stress with your mind. My aim in this book is to direct your body's response to tension and teach you how to relax, and also to enhance your resistance to stress so that the ill effects do not accumulate.

What do we mean by stress?

In physics, stress means a force or pressure that produces some kind of deformation or strain, and this is a useful definition to remember. When we think of stress, we do think of it as something that produces harmful results. In everyday language, stress is anything that is perceived by us as a burden or pressure, but individuals react differently and one person's burden may be another's enjoyable challenge.

Stress can be externally induced, for example by cold, heat, pain or noise, or internally by feelings such as worry, fear, grief, or excitement. Although the stressors (things that cause stress) for each individual may be different, our stress mechanisms will respond in much the same way.

Reactions to stress

The body's response to stress is known as the "fight or flight" reaction. Thousands of years ago, fleeing or fighting was the only sensible response to the stressors of our ancestors whose lives were threatened daily. Although the way we live now bears little comparison to our ancestors" environment, our bodies and our response to stress remain the same. When we feel we are being threatened or are under pressure, hormones are released into the bloodstream that prepare the body for action. They cause, for example, your heart to pump faster, your breathing to quicken, your body to perspire, your digestion to slow down or stop, your liver to release glucose to produce extra energy and your blood to be diverted toward your muscles. These are normal and useful reactions, but when they go on too long or are inappropriate, they lead to problems. When stress is sustained or when fighting or fleeing is an inappropriate response—as it is to the kind of stress we tend to face in the modern world—then stress will adversely affect your body and your mind.

It is vital to be aware of your own body and to notice if stress is affecting you. Physical reactions range from palpitations, dry mouth, sweating, shallow rapid breathing and jaw clenching to fatigue, muscular aches and pains, headaches, indigestion, diarrhoea or constipation, insomnia and spots. Emotional signs include an inability to relax, feeling under pressure, feeling mentally tired, being easily irritated or tearful, finding it difficult to concentrate, restlessness and fidgeting, pessimism, becoming fearful or indecisive, being unable to find pleasure, mood swings, and changes in eating patterns. You need to watch out for these signs and deal with them in order to avoid long-term harm and ill-health.

Movement and posture

The key to well-being is physical activity, of the right sort. It is also one of the solutions to dealing with the problems of stress. Activity is vital to life: all muscles benefit from movement and this in turn enhances good blood flow and helps circulation. Movement induces relaxation because muscle groups

work in pairs—while one group is contracting the opposing group is relaxing—but muscles held tight and tense in contraction for long periods impede circulation, which can cause the muscle to go into a cramp-like spasm. This prolonged tension will make you more tired than you should be and result in muscular aches, headache, backache, and tender knots all over the body. Your body has a finely balanced system of almost 600 skeletal muscles designed to be active, but when this system becomes imbalanced, your posture suffers.

Every part of the body, from the skin and muscles down to our ligaments and bones, is subject to strains caused by stress-induced poor posture, but it is the back that takes most of the burden of stress. Instead of standing or sitting with the curves of the spine in proportion to each other, stress tends to cause an increase or decrease in the curves at the neck, mid-back and lower back. As a response to stress, people tend either to stiffen and stand ramrod-straight or allow their bodies to sag and stoop, both of which have dire consequences. Perhaps you are even now slouching forward in a chair or over a table with your shoulders hunched and your legs crossed tightly or your hands clenched. The exercises in this book will help you recognize when you are adapting your posture and notice the areas being strained and will also prevent or relieve such strains in the future.

Exercise and health

Everywhere today people are learning for themselves the benefits of movement, both for the mind and the body. We are discovering that active people are more resistant to illness, have greater stamina to get them through hard times and gain an overall feeling of well-being. This develops confidence and a resistance to stress and therefore they are less likely to get depressed or tense. Exercise is also an effective means of releasing the tension that can lead to mental and physical ills.

The body has an innate intelligence that is always striving for health: that is, given the proper opportunity, the body will try to repair, regenerate and renew in an effort to maintain itself, and we can actively help this. Any input you direct toward your well-being, whether it is starting exercise, modifying your diet or stopping smoking, is quickly rewarded by the body's ability to respond positively. And with exercise, it doesn't matter how little you have

exercised in the past or how sedentary your present lifestyle, improvement is possible at any age; the opportunity to better our health is available to each one of us.

Good health is more than just the absence of disease. It is a dynamic state that allows people to thrive and adapt to the stresses they find in their environment without harm. Our bodies are constantly sending out messages of *di*-stress and it is up to us to listen and take responsibility for our own lives. Embarking on a program of gentle exercises is an excellent way of doing this.

Guidelines for exercising

The exercises in this book have been drawn from a background of yoga, dance, osteopathy and natural movement, and are all non-impact and gentle on the cardio-vascular system—the heart and circulation. Many of them are stretches which will keep your muscles supple and are a good preparation for more vigorous exercise, but they are not in themselves— and should not be—too vigorous. The important thing to remember is that when you exercise correctly it feels good. There should be no pain involved. I certainly don't follow the maxim "no pain, no gain": exercise and stretching are not a form of torture to atone for not living a healthy lifestyle, so do not expect them to hurt as some kind of punishment. Be gentle to your body and it will respond. Listen to the messages your body is giving you.

Do not set yourself limits and try to exceed them every time you exercise. Nor should exercising be a personal contest with yourself or anybody else: it should be fitted to your own personal needs, since everyone has different degrees of tension in different muscle groups around the body. The goal is to reduce tension and relieve stress, not to achieve extreme flexibility, which causes overstretching and injury.

Who can exercise?

Anyone can do these movements, whether he or she wants to relieve stress in general or to work on specific areas of tension. The exercises are not dependent on age, sex, general fitness or suppleness and require no previous experience. The methods are very gentle and have been designed so as to suit individual differences in tension and flexibility, so if you are generally healthy you can begin them straight away. If you are undergoing medical treatment or have a history of cardio-vascular, pulmonary (breathing) or degenerative problems, seek the advice of a medical practitioner before starting. These exercises are also safe (upon the advice of your physician) to do in the first six months of an uncomplicated pregnancy, if you follow the instructions correctly. However, in pregnancy the body begins to release hormones designed to allow the pelvis to stretch during childbirth. These affect all the ligaments, so take extra care in the last three months when doing the stretching exercises, and seek medical advice.

It is possible that you may feel some mild discomfort following the first few sessions of exercising. These areas of tenderness should not persist or cause you any acute pain. If the discomfort is severe or persistent, seek medical advice before continuing. It may be that the exercises are highlighting an area that has been tense and restricted for a long period and needs specialist attention. In this case, you might consult an osteopath, who will try to solve the problem.

Time and space, equipment and clothing

These exercises can be done anywhere at any time. Indeed some, particularly the Quick Relaxers on pages 62-72, are designed to be done even in the somewhat unfavorable environment of the office or workplace. Of course it would be ideal if we could free some time and space in peaceful surroundings and a relaxed atmosphere on a daily basis, and focus our energies on an exercise routine. But it can be difficult to isolate a certain amount of time each day—trying to do this can be stressful in itself. So have realistic expectations of what you can and can't do, and try to fit your exercises in whenever you have some free time or whenever you feel the need for some stress relief. It is far better to do five minutes of relaxed, unhurried movement than to whiz through as many exercises as you can in 20 minutes.

There are times when these gentle movements are particularly useful, such as before and after any particularly stressful period or any vigorous physical activity. It is also good to get into the habit of exercising in the morning to prepare yourself for the day ahead and in the evening to release the tension that has built up during the day.

Apart from everyday items such as a chair, stool, pillow, or cushion and enough floorspace with a soft covering such as a carpet or rug, you don't need any special

equipment. Wear comfortable clothing that is loose or stretchy enough to allow you unrestricted freedom of movement.

Working through the exercises

The book is divided into sections, beginning with warm-up exercises to get your circulation moving, then exercises that relax your whole body, followed by movements that relax particular areas of the body where tension accumulates, such as the head, neck, shoulders, back, hands, and feet. There is a is a section on quick stress-relieving exercises that can be performed at the workplace and one on how to control your breathing to release tension. There are relaxing massages to do by yourself or with a partner; mental techniques, such as visualization, that soothe away stress; and a section on nutrition, detailing how to eat well to reduce stress. However, there is no particular order in which the exercises should be done, and I suggest you have a look at them all and begin with those that seem to fit your needs. The exercises are adjustable to the individual and can be done separately or in their entirety, though you shouldn't do them all at once without building up to this, slowly.

To start, read and re-read all the instructions for each exercise until they are clear, and use the book to prompt you through the various stages; with time and practice just looking at the picture will enable you to do the whole exercise. Note if there are any cautions or contra-indications that are relevant to you. For safety, there are a few general rules to follow:

- Ease into the exercises slowly with no sudden movements.
- Count out the seconds as you hold the position. Do not go on for longer than specified.
- With stretches, do not bounce back and forth in an effort to stretch further. It should be a sustained effort.
- Make sure you have something to support you nearby in case you lose your balance.
- Breathe slowly in a gentle rhythmic manner. Never hold your breath.
- If you feel any pain, discomfort, dizziness or nausea, stop the exercise and move to a resting position.
- Do not perform the exercises under the influence of alcohol, drugs, or painkillers. Your body is less sensitive and you are more likely to cause damage to yourself.

Bearing these rules in mind, try the different techniques in this book and keep experimenting, using them in different combinations. For example, do some breathing exercises before you stretch for a while and end with some relaxation techniques and massage. You may feel happy working with a partner or you may find the solitude of relaxing on your own more rewarding. Each individual has different perceptions of stress and will find some techniques suit them more than others.

This book should give you an insight into the mechanisms involved in stress and the effect it has on your body and mind but it should also empower you with the ability to control your response to stress. This is a subtle change of perception that will greatly enhance your quality and appreciation of life. The secret of relaxation is to keep practicing until it is a way of being, so that it is as natural as breathing. There are many ways of finding your own personal peace. This doesn't mean that you have to withdraw from the world or turn away from problems. Far from it. This book, I hope, will give you the encouragement to face the stresses of life and to develop your own coping techniques that will give you stability, control and, ultimately, freedom.

UP AND DOWN

It is a good idea to do the warm-up exercises here and on pages 14-17 one after the other. They are excellent for getting your joints and your circulation moving. If you "let yourself go" and allow gravity to play its part in achieving a rhythm you will find your whole body becoming more and more relaxed.

1 Stand with your feet a shoulders' width apart and your knees slightly bent, with your arms hanging loosely by your sides.

2 Keeping your arms parallel to your body and moving them together, swing them in front and then behind you in a slow, easy rhythm.

3 Build up the momentum by allowing your knees to bend and straighten with each swing.

4 Increase the impetus of the swings
  by involving your whole body, so
that your arms are reaching up
overhead at the top of the swing
and your body is bent forward with
your arms behind your back
at the bottom of the swing.

5 Maintain the movement for 20
  to 30 seconds, then gradually
decrease the momentum until you
are standing still.

SIDE TO SIDE

As your arms are swinging, be aware of the feeling of letting go of a weight at the lowest point of the swing and a sense of lightness at the top. Allow your body the freedom to enjoy the upward stretches.

1 Stand with your feet wider than a shoulders' width apart and your knees slightly bent, with your arms held loosely down in front of you.

2 Slowly swing your arms from side to side in front of you, gradually increasing the extent of the swings until the momentum takes your hands up to shoulder height.

3 Build up the momentum by allowing your knees to bend and straighten with each swing. Let your head turn with each swing and follow the movement of your hands with your eyes.

4 Allow your arms to lift higher at the end of each swing and, as each swing broadens, feel your body weight shift accordingly from side to side. As your arms reach up on one side let the heel on the opposite side lift.

5 Maintain the movement for 20 to 30 seconds, then gradually decrease the momentum until you are standing still.

BACK AND FORTH

As with the other warm-up exercises, if you let the force of gravity help your arms to move freely and rhythmically, your body relaxes—almost in spite of itself.

1 Stand with your feet a shoulders' width apart and your knees slightly bent, with your arms hanging loosely by your sides.

2 Lift one arm forward in front of you and the other arm straight out behind you. Allow your arms to swing easily by your sides in opposite directions, forward and backward.

3 Build up the momentum by allowing your knees to bend and straighten with each swing.

4 Twist your shoulders with each swing, and allow your head to rock, bending it to the left when the left arm swings to the front and to the right when the right arm is in front.

5 To open the movement even further, now turn your head from side to side, so that you are looking behind you at the end of each arm swing.

6 Maintain the movement for 20 to 30 seconds, then gradually decrease the momentum until you are standing still.

REACH OUT

This is a gentle stretching exercise that will begin to awaken your body.

1 Stand with your feet a shoulders' width apart and your arms hanging loosely by your side.

2 Clench your fists for a moment and then relax them.

3 Raise your arms and reach straight out in front of you. Clench your fists and then relax them.

4 Move your arms to the sides at shoulder height, with your palms facing downward. Reach out, then clench your fists and then relax them.

5 Now raise your arms overhead with the palms facing inward. Reach straight up, then clench your fists and then relax them.

6 Repeat steps 1 to 5 three times.

BODY CIRCLES

These slow rhythmic circles loosen your whole body and particularly help relax the muscles around your waist.

1 Stand with your feet a shoulders' width apart and raise your arms overhead with your palms facing inward. Keep your knees slightly bent.

2 Keeping your feet still, your body upright and your arms up, slowly move your body in a circle, using your hips. Continue circling in one direction for 20-30 seconds.

3 Repeat step 2, circling in the other direction.

4 Repeat steps 2-3 three times.

REACH UP

In this exercise a feeling of looseness spreads from your sides up and down your body as you reach around and up.

1 Stand with your feet slightly more than a shoulders' width apart and your knees slightly bent.

2 Keeping your feet still, slowly twist your upper body as if you are trying to look over your left shoulder, reaching up with your left arm and bending your right arm diagonally across your chest.

3 Hold the position for five seconds and repeat in the opposite direction.

4 Repeat steps 2-3 three times.

FLEXING

Here you can feel your body—especially your spine—gaining flexibility from the contrasting movements.

1 Kneel down and place your hands palms down on the floor, directly under your shoulders. Make sure your knees are in line with your hands.

2 Hang your head down toward your chest, relaxing your neck, and slowly ease your pelvis downward. Try to form an arch toward the ceiling with your back. Hold this position for five seconds.

3 Now allow the middle of your spine to sag toward the floor and encourage this movement by gently moving your head toward your back and letting your pelvis move upward. Hold this position for five seconds.

4 Repeat steps 2-3 three times.

Try to balance your breathing so that it becomes part of the movement. Breathe in as you arch your back and breathe out as you allow your spine to sag.

HOLD AND RELEASE

It may take a while to coordinate all the actions of this exercise at the same time, so I recommend doing each in turn and getting used to how they feel and so becoming rigid gradually. When you are familiar with the feeling, you can contract all these muscle groups together at the same time.

1 Lie on your back with your head on a pillow, a cushion under your knees and your arms by your side

2 Push your head back into the pillow as hard as you can.

3 Reach down with your arms and clench your fists.

4 Clench your buttocks together.

5 Bend your feet up toward you, keeping your heels on the ground and your knees bent.

6 Hold your entire body rigid for five to ten seconds. Then release the tension and relax, taking a few slow, deep breaths and lie still for a while.

SIDE STRETCH

These movements gently stretch out and then relax the muscles along your sides.

1 Lie flat on your back with your head on a pillow and your arms by your sides.

2 Roll over onto your left shoulder and side, with the lower part of your left arm lying comfortably in front of you and bending your left knee so that the lower part of your left leg lies behind you.

3 Reach up behind your head with your right arm and stretch down in front of your body with your right leg. Feel the gentle pull, especially along the side of your torso, and hold for five seconds.

4 Now bring your knees and your elbows into your chest and curl up your body into a ball. Hold this position for five seconds.

5 Roll over onto your back. Do steps 1 to 4, moving onto your right side and stretching your left arm and leg.

6 Repeat steps 1 to 5 three times.

SPIRAL STRETCH

This exercise creates a stretch spiraling through your whole body. Try to imagine you are reaching beyond the tips of your fingers and your toes to achieve the fullest stretch.

1 Lie flat on your back with your head resting on a pillow, your arms by your sides and your knees bent so that your feet are flat on the floor.

2 Move your right arm overhead, reaching up with your hand, and at the same time push your left leg down flat on the floor, pointing your toes away from you.

3 Stretch out your arm and your leg as far as you can for ten seconds and then relax, bringing your right hand down beside your body and your left knee up.

4 Now do steps 2 to 3 with your left arm and right leg.

5 Repeat steps 1 to 5 three times.

LENGTHENING

Try to feel every part of your body growing longer as you stretch out as far as you can.

1 Lie flat on your back with your head resting on a pillow, your arms by your sides and your knees bent so that your feet are flat on the floor

2 Raise both arms overhead and reach back as far as you can while at the same time straightening both legs pressing down onto the floor, pointing your toes down and away from you.

3 Hold the stretch for ten seconds and then relax, bringing you knees up and your arms down by your sides.

4 Repeat steps 2 and 3 three times.

MOUTH RELAXER

These exaggerated grimaces help release the muscles around your mouth which can become tense with stress.

1 Move the corners of your mouth up into a big smile and hold for five seconds.

2 Pull the corners of your mouth back and down, tensing the muscles at the front of the neck, and hold for five seconds.

3 Relax and then repeat steps 1 and 2 three times.

For all the face exercises here and overleaf, sit comfortably on a chair or with your legs crossed on the floor, you hands resting lightly on your knees or legs and your shoulders loose. Remove glasses before starting.

JAW RELAXER

The jaw can easily become stiff with tension. These movements keep it loose.

1 With your lips apart, move your jaw forward so that your lower teeth are in front of your upper teeth. Hold for five seconds and return to the normal position.

2 Now move your jaw to the left, holding for five seconds, and then to the right, holding for another five seconds.

3 Repeat steps 1 and 2 three times.

If your jaw clicks, or you feel discomfort moving it around, do not do this exercise.

FACE LOOSENER

These contrasting movements loosen tense muscles and energize the whole face.

1 With your mouth closed or very slightly open, clench your teeth and hold for five seconds.

2 Now open your mouth as wide as you can and hold for five seconds.

3 Repeat steps 1 and 2 three times.

STRETCHING

These gentle movements stretch the whole neck, from head to shoulder on each side.

1 Sit comfortably on a chair or with your legs crossed on the floor, with your arms hanging or resting loosely by your sides.

2 Slowly lean your head toward your left shoulder as far as you can without straining.

3 Reach over with your left hand and lightly clasp the left side of your head. Take a slow, deep breath in and out and relax for a few moments, feeling the gentle stretch along the left side of your neck.

4 Release your head and let your arm rest down by your side. Raise your head and repeat steps 2 and 3, but leaning toward your right shoulder and using your right hand.

5 Repeat steps 2 to 4 three times.

Do not pull your head toward your shoulder with your hand; just let it rest lightly on your head. There should be no feeling of strain.

FLEXING

This exercise stretches the muscles at the front and back of your neck, loosening any tension.

1 Sit comfortably on a chair or with your legs crossed on the floor, with your arms hanging or resting loosely by your sides. Keep your shoulders down and relaxed throughout the exercise.

2 Move your chin down toward your chest as far as you can comfortably go and hold for five seconds.

3 Slowly move you head up and backward as far as is comfortable and hold for five seconds, looking up at the ceiling or sky.

4 Repeat steps 2 and 3 three times.

Make sure that any movement is coming from you neck and not your back. Keep your back still with no arching or rounding.

NECK RELAXER

This is a fast and effective way of relaxing the muscles at the base of your head which stress can make tense and tight.

1 Sit comfortably on a chair or with your legs crossed on the floor, with your arms hanging or resting loosely by your sides. Keep your shoulders down and relaxed throughout the exercise.

2 Move your head down slightly by pressing your chin back onto your neck and hold for five seconds.

3 Keeping your chin on your neck, gently push the back of your head backward and upward and hold for five seconds. Raise your head and relax.

4 Repeat steps 2 and 3 three times.

EASING

These movements ease tense muscles at the side of the neck and the top of the shoulders.

1 Sit comfortably on a chair or with your legs crossed on the floor, with your arms hanging or resting loosely by your sides.

2 Interlace your fingers and lightly clasp your hands behind your neck, with your elbows pointing out sideways.

3 Gently lean your neck to one side and hold for five seconds, then lean to the opposite side and hold for five seconds.

4 Repeat step 3 three times.

MOBILIZING

This is an excellent exercise if your neck is stiff from tension—feel your neck becoming more mobile as you gently turn your head.

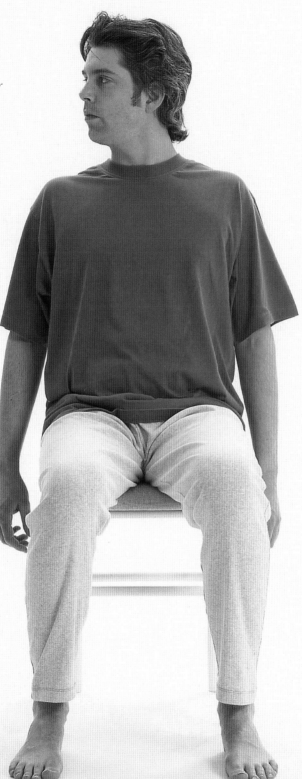

1 Sit comfortably on a chair or with your legs crossed on the floor, with your arms hanging or resting loosely by your sides.

2 Slowly turn your head as far as you can comfortably reach so that you are looking over your right shoulder. Close your left eye and hold the position without straining for five seconds.

3 Open your eye and gently turn your head in the opposite direction, looking over your left shoulder, closing your right eye and holding for five seconds.

4 Open your eye and turn your head to look straight ahead. Sit relaxed for about 30 seconds.

5 Repeat steps 2 to 4 three times.

If you feel dizzy or sick at any point during this exercise stop immediately.

REACHING BEHIND

These movements ease stiffness in the shoulders and upper arms. Initially you may find that you can reach further up or down more comfortably with one hand, which means that the relevant shoulder is more flexible.

1 Stand straight with your feet a shoulders' width apart and your arms loosely by your sides.

2 Raise both arms over and behind your head and reach down your back as far as you can for five seconds.

3 Lower your arms and bend them behind your back, with the back of the hands against your back, and reach up as far as you can for five seconds.

4 Repeat steps 2 and 3 three times.

CURVING

As you do this exercise, you can feel your shoulder joints slowly freeing themselves.

1 Stand straight with your feet a shoulders' width apart and your arms loosely by your sides.

2 Bring your hands up against your shoulders with your palms facing toward you. Draw your elbows together against your body so that they touch. Hold for ten seconds and then lower your hands.

3 Bring your hands up against your shoulders with your palms facing outward. Draw your elbows together against your body so that they touch. Hold for ten seconds and then lower your hands.

4 Repeat steps 2 and 3 three times.

The closer you can keep your elbows tucked into your body, the more effective this exercise will be.

WINDMILLS

You can shake off the tension in your shoulders with this invigorating exercise.

1 Stand straight with your feet a shoulders' width apart and your arms loosely by your sides.

2 Raise one arm overhead and bring it forward and down and then up behind to make a large circle. Start circling in the same way with the other arm, alternating arms so that when one comes down the other is moving up—a little like swimming the front crawl.

3 Continue circling vigorously for about 30 seconds and then slow down and stop.

4 Repeat the circles in the same way but in a backward direction, as if swimming the backstroke. Continue for about 30 seconds and then slow down and stop.

5 Repeat steps 2 and 3 once more.

This exercise is enjoyable and you may want to repeat it more than once, but be sure that you always finish with backward circles.

DIAGONAL STRETCH

This open stretch helps loosen all the muscles surrounding your shoulders.

1 Stand straight with your feet a shoulders' width apart and your arms loosely by your sides.

2 Raise your left arm and reach up and slightly away from you while reaching down and slightly away from you with your right arm. Hold for five seconds.

3 Repeat the movements with opposite arms and hold for five seconds.

4 Repeat steps 2 and 3 three times.

ROTATING

These movements encourage stiff shoulders to regain their full range of movement.

1 Stand straight with your feet a shoulders' width apart and your arms loosely by your sides.

2 Move your arms up by your sides at shoulder height and bend both arms at the elbow so that the lower arm hangs straight down with your palms facing behind you.

3 Keeping your upper arms horizontal, push your hands behind you as far as they will go and hold for five seconds.

4 With the elbow as a pivot, rotate both arms upward until your palms are facing forward and then press your hands back as far as they will go and hold for five seconds and then rotate your lower arms down again.

5 Repeat steps 3 and 4 three times, feeling the stretch at the top of your shoulders.

PULLING

These contrasting movements relieve tension in the front and back of the shoulders.

1 Stand straight with your feet a shoulders' width apart and your arms loosely by your sides.

2 Pull your shoulders forward as far as they will go. Your arms will roll inward, but make sure that the movement comes from the shoulders not the arms. Hold for ten seconds.

3 Pull your shoulders backward and feel your shoulder blades move towards your spine. Hold for 15 seconds and then relax.

4 Repeat steps 3 and 4 three times.

Try to keep your head still and upright throughout this exercise.

CLENCH AND STRETCH

Tension can build up quickly in your hands and, unnoticed, spread up through the arms to your neck and head. This exercise makes you focus on the tension in your hands and forearms so that you enjoy the release as you stretch.

1 Sit comfortably and rest your hands in front of you on your knees or on the arms of a chair with your palms facing upward.

2 Clench you fists tightly and hold for ten seconds.

3 Relax your hands and then stretch out your fingers, pointing them away from you, and hold for ten seconds.

4 Repeat steps 2 and 3 three times.

WRIST FLEXER

These movements release tension in your wrists and increase their mobility.

1 Sit or stand comfortably and raise your arms to shoulder height. Bring your hands together with your palms and fingers touching and your fingers pointing upward. Hold for ten seconds and then relax your arms.

2 Raise your arms to shoulder height and bring the backs of your hands together with your fingers pointing straight downward. Hold for ten seconds and then relax.

If you feel any discomfort on the back or front of your wrist at any time, stop the exercise.

UPPER ARM STRETCHER

This gentle stretch releases tension along the back of your arm between the shoulder and elbow.

1 Sit or stand comfortably and, with your right arm, reach up over your head and down your back.

2 Raise your left arm and hold onto your right, just behind the elbow. Pull lightly on your right arm for five seconds so that you feel a gentle stretch and then relax both arms.

3 Repeat the movement with the opposite arms, so that your right arm helps your left to stretch.

4 Repeat steps 1 to 3 three times.

UPPER ARM RELEASE

This is an alternative way to release tension in your upper arm.

1 Stand or sit comfortably and reach across to the back of your right shoulder with your left arm.

2 With your right hand, hold onto your left arm at or just behind the elbow, and gently pull the arm to the left to help the stretch. Hold for five seconds and then relax both arms.

3 Repeat the movement with the opposite arms, so that your left arm helps your right to stretch.

4 Repeat steps 1 to 3 three times.

HAND MOBILIZER

This gentle circling movement helps mobilize stiff hands and wrists.

1 Stand comfortably with your arms hanging down a little way out from your sides.

2 Bend your hands up from the wrists so that your palms face the floor. Push your fingers up and bend them a little.

3 Slowly rotate your hands at the wrists inward toward your body, dropping your palms down at the innermost point then bringing them up again so that your hands make a complete rotation. Keep circling for three complete rotations.

4 Now slowly rotate your hands at the wrists outward away from your body, dropping your palms down at the outermost point then bringing them up again so that your hands make a complete rotation. Keep circling for three complete rotations.

5 Relax with your arms hanging loosely by your sides for 30 seconds.

6 Repeat steps 1 to 4 three times.

SIDEWAYS STRETCH

*This exercise gives a relaxing sensation of
expansion in the ribcage.*

1 Stand with your feet a shoulders'
width apart and place both hands
behind your head.

2 Without moving your head forward,
slowly move one elbow downward
while moving the other up. Feel a
gentle stretch in your side and hold
for five seconds.

3 Repeat step 2 but on the opposite
side.

4 Repeat steps 2 and 3 three times.

Try not to move your lower
torso: the movement should
all be above the waist.

CHEST STRETCHER

These movements give a refreshing open sensation across your chest as you gently stretch your pectoral muscles in three different positions.

1 Stand about one to two feet (or half a meter) away from an open door frame, with one foot slightly in front of the other, and place your hands on it at head height.

2 Lean into the doorway so that you feel a gentle stretch across your chest. Hold for five seconds.

3 With your hands placed on the doorframe above head height, repeat steps 1 and 2 and then repeat again with your hands below head height.

4 Repeat steps 1 to 3 three times.

UPPER BACK STRETCHER

Feel the tension in your back slip away as this exercise softly lengthens the top of your spine.

1 Sit comfortably on the floor with your legs crossed and your arms by your sides. Let your head come forward so that your chin is resting on the front of your neck.

2 With your palms facing backward, stretch your arms back and up behind you as far as they will go. Hold the position for five seconds and then relax your arms and raise your head.

3 Repeat steps 1 and 2 three times.

LOWER BACK STRETCHER

Stress can often cause painful tension to accumulate in the lower back.
This is a very gentle and effective way of stretching and soothing the area.

1 Lie on your back on a comfortable surface
with your head on a cushion. Bend your
knees and separate them so that they are a
shoulders' width apart.

2 Draw first one knee and then the other
toward your chest. Put your hands across
your knees and gently pull them as close as
possible to your chest. Keep this soft pressure
for about 30 seconds and then relax, letting
go of your knees and placing your feet on
the floor.

3 Repeat step 2 three times.

You must feel comfortable
doing this exercise: if you
find the floor hurts your
spine, try doing it on a
softer surface such as a
mat or even a firm bed.

SPINE LENGTHENER

Try to "let yourself go" and relax fully so that gravity can play its part in helping the spine stretch out.

1 Sit on a chair that is comfortable and at the right height for you. Your thighs should be roughly parallel to the floor and your feet flat on the floor.

2 Separate your knees so that they and your feet are a shoulders' width apart, with your feet facing forward.

3 Slowly lean forward and down and let your hands rest alongside your feet. Allow your head to hang loosely between your knees without any strain on your neck muscles.

4 Remain in this position for 30 seconds, then very slowly raise your body to sit upright.

5 Repeat steps 3 and 4 three times.

If you begin to feel dizzy or sick with your head between your knees, carefully sit upright and don't continue with the exercise.

SIDE STRETCHER 1

The exercises here and on pages 51 and 52 will ease tension and increase flexibility in each side of the lower body. They are progressive and should be done in sequence as they appear here.

1 Stand with your feet together and knees slightly bent. Place your hands on your hips.

2 Lean to one side keeping your hips perfectly still. Feel the stretch along the side of your body and hold for ten seconds.

3 Now lean to the other side and hold for ten seconds.

4 Repeat steps 2 and 3 three times.

SIDE STRETCHER 2

*This stretch continues to reduce stiffness
and increase flexibility.*

1 Stand with your feet a shoulders'
width apart and knees slightly
bent. Place your right hand on
your head and your left hand on
your hip.

2 Lean to the left and allow your
right hip to lift slightly as the
left hip moves in. Feel the stretch
along the right side of your body
and hold for ten seconds.

3 Repeat the movement in the
opposite direction, placing your
left hand on your head and your
right on your hip, and hold for ten
seconds.

4 Repeat steps 2 and 3 three times.

SIDE STRETCHER 3

This wide stretch further opens up movement along your sides.

1 Stand with your feet wide apart and your knees slightly bent. Raise your right arm straight overhead and place your left hand on your hip.

2 Lean as far to the left as you can. Feel a wide stretch along the right side of your body and hold for ten seconds.

3 Repeat the movement in the opposite direction, with your left hand overhead and your right on your hip, and hold for ten seconds.

4 Repeat steps 2 and 3 three times.

SPIRAL TWIST

These gentle twisting movements stretch out and free the lower part of the spine.

1 Sit with your feet wider than a shoulders' width apart, in a chair that is comfortable and at the right height for you. Your thighs should be roughly parallel to the floor and your feet flat on the floor.

2 Place a long stick behind your head, lightly resting along the top of your shoulders, and hold on to the ends.

3 Slowly turn your upper body to one side and try to lift it as you turn. Turn only from the waist and don't slump forward: if you keep your lower body still and your upper body lightly pulled up, you will feel a wonderful lengthening stretch at the base of your spine as you turn. Hold the stretch for five seconds.

4 Repeat the movements in step 3 but turn to the opposite side. Turn back to the front and rest for 30 seconds.

5 Repeat steps 3 and 4 three times.

BACK-OF-LEG EXTENDER

This excellent exercise not only stretches the leg but also releases tension in the back and is good for keeping lower back pain at bay.

1 Stand facing a stool or chair, and have another chair next to your left side with its back toward you. Place your left hand on the back of the chair for support.

2 Place your right heel on the stool, keeping your knee slightly bent and point your toes toward you. This position should feel comfortable, so make sure the stool is not too high.

3 Gently lean your body forward and feel a light, relaxing stretch along the back of your right leg. Hold for 20 seconds.

4 Move the stool and turn around so that you are supporting yourself with your right hand, with the stool in front of you. Repeat steps 2 and 3 with your left leg.

5 Repeat steps 2 to 4 three times.

If you find a chair or stool is too high for comfort, start by using a lower surface to rest your leg on, gradually raising the level as you get used to the exercise and feel more comfortable.

HIP EXPANDER

If you relax into this stretch you will feel the front of your hips gradually expanding and feeling free.

1 Rest on your right knee with your left foot flat on the floor, well in front of you. Have a chair on your left, placing your left hand on it for support. Keep your lower right leg stretched directly out behind you and your upper body upright, looking straight ahead.

2 Gradually and smoothly move your body forward as far as you can while keeping your upper body upright. Feel the loosening stretch along the front of your right hip and hold for ten seconds.

3 Bring your body back and relax for about 30 seconds. Turn around and repeat steps 1 and 2 on the opposite side, stretching your left hip.

4 Repeat steps 1 to 3 three times.

INNER THIGH STRETCHER

This gentle exercise gives a lovely feeling of tension release along the inside of your thighs.

1 Sit on the floor and place the soles of your feet against each other in front of you as near to your body as is comfortable.

2 Rest your hands lightly on your knees and let your knees sag downward. Feel the stretch loosening your inner thighs. Hold for ten seconds, then bring your knees together and relax.

3 Repeat steps 1 and 2 three times.

Do not push your knees down with your hands. This is a gentle stretch and there should be no feeling of strain.

FRONT-OF-THIGH STRETCHER

This exercise creates a long relaxing stretch up and down your thighs.

1 Lie down on your front on a soft surface with your legs straight, resting your head on your left side.

2 Bend your right knee and draw the back of your heel straight up toward your right buttock.

3 Hold onto your foot with your right hand and gently pull your heel straight back toward you. Feel the stretch all along the front of your thigh and hold for ten seconds.

4 Let your leg go back down and turn your head to your right side. Repeat steps 2 and 3 with your left leg and hand.

5 Repeat steps 2 to 4 three times.

OUTER THIGH STRETCHER

As this exercise gently stretches your thigh you can feel a wonderful release of tension in your hips.

1 Stand about two to three feet (or a meter) away from a wall, sideways on, with your feet together and your knees slightly bent.

2 Place your right hand or lean your right forearm against the wall at shoulder height.

3 Slowly push your hips toward the wall and feel the stretch all along the outside of your right thigh up to your hip. Hold for 20 seconds.

4 Turn around and repeat steps 1 to 3 on your left side.

5 Repeat steps 1 to 4 three times.

CALF STRETCHER

Release the tension in the back of your legs with this gentle stretch.

1 Stand about one to two feet (or half a meter) away from a wall, facing it, and place your hands against the wall at head height.

2 Move one foot a further one to two feet (or half a meter) behind you. Keep your toes pointing forward and both feet flat on the floor.

3 Slowly lean into the wall, making sure that the heel of your back foot does not come off the floor, and feel the tension in your back leg flow away as the calf muscle stretches. Hold for 20 seconds.

4 Bring your feet together and repeat steps 2 and 3 with your other leg.

5 Repeat steps 2 to 4 three times.

FOOT FLEXER

This exercise frees the movement in your feet and helps the tension flow away from your lower legs to your toes.

1 Sit comfortably on the floor or on a low cushion with your legs straight out in front of you.

2 Point your toes away from you as far as you can and hold the stretch for 15 seconds.

3 Draw your toes back up toward you, keeping your legs straight, and feel the difference in the stretch. Hold for 15 seconds.

4 Repeat steps 2 and 3 three times.

If you begin to feel a cramping sensation in your calves, stop the exercise.

ANKLE ROLLS

These loosening circles relax stiff ankle joints.

1 Stand with your feet together and place your hands on your knees.

2 Slowly move your knees in a circular motion, keeping your feet as still as possible so that the movement comes from the ankles, as if the ankles were a pivot.

3 Continue for 20 seconds and then circle in the opposite direction for 20 seconds.

4 Repeat steps 2 and 3 three times.

FACE RELIEVER

If your face feels tight this easy exercise will relax the muscles around the cheeks, mouth, and jaw. Like all the Quick Relaxers, it's a good one to do at work, though you may have to reassure colleagues about your odd facial expressions!

1 Sit comfortably on a chair or on the floor.

2 Suck in your cheeks and push your lips forward. Hold for ten seconds.

3 Blow air into your cheeks keeping your mouth closed. Hold for ten seconds.

4 Repeat steps 2 and 3 three times.

FOREHEAD SMOOTHER

Stress can cause the muscles in your forehead to tense up and leads to headaches. Clear those worry lines and banish the headache with these contrasting movements.

1 Bring your eyebrows together in a frown and close your eyes. Hold for ten seconds.

2 Now raise your eyebrows as high as you can and open your eyes wide. Hold for ten seconds.

3 Repeat steps 1 and 2 three times.

SHOULDER ROLLS

Tension often causes stiffness in joints. This flowing circular motion improves the flexibility of the shoulders as well as relaxing them.

1 Sit cross-legged, or stand or sit with your feet and knees apart. Push one shoulder forward and pull the other back, but keep your body facing forward.

2 Roll the shoulders forward, alternately moving the front shoulder back and the back shoulder forward. Continue in a smooth, continuous rhythm for about 30 seconds.

3 Now reverse the direction of the circling and roll the shoulders backward in the same way for a further 30 seconds.

4 Repeat steps 2 and 3 three times.

SHOULDER SHRUGS

This exercise releases tension in the neck and shoulders and helps you breathe away stress. If you are working or concentrating hard, stress can build up without your noticing: feeling the variation between these two positions helps you become aware of the difference between tension and relaxation so that you can recognize when you are becoming tense and thus deliberately relax.

1 Sit cross-legged, or stand or sit with your feet and knees apart. Keep your head up and your shoulders back, and let your arms hang loosely by your side.

2 Take a deep breath in and as you do so, raise both shoulders toward your ears. Hold this position, maintaining the tension in your shoulders, for five seconds.

3 Slowly let your breath out, allow your shoulders to sag down to their resting position and relax.

4 Repeat steps 2 and 3 three times.

NECK RELAXER

This is a very positive, natural movement that not only gently lengthens your neck but gives an overall feeling of well-being. Do this often if you are working or concentrating hard, especially at a desk.

1 Sit cross-legged, or stand or sit with your feet and knees apart.

2 Interlace your fingers and clasp the back of your head just above your neck. Point your elbows out to the sides.

3 Very gently tilt your head backward and feel your neck stretching out. Hold for five seconds.

Stop if you feel any discomfort at the base of your neck during this exercise.

CHEST STRETCHER

If you are tense you may become aware of a tight feeling in your chest which you can quickly relieve with this exercise.

1 Stand one to two feet (or half a meter) away from the corner of a room, facing into the angle. Place your hands at head height on the adjoining walls.

2 Move one foot back and lean into the corner. Feel the stretch opening up and relaxing your chest and hold for five seconds.

3 If you like, and if you have time, try the stretch with your hands placed higher and then lower to open up the chest in different ways. Experiment with your hand positions to gain maximum effect.

4 Repeat steps 2 and 3 three times.

SPINE SPIRAL

In this exercise, if you lift your upper body lightly as you turn you will feel a wonderful lengthening stretch at the base of your spine that will loosen and relax it. These are good movements to do if you have been sitting for a long time.

1 Sit back in your chair with your feet placed wide apart. Keep your feet still during the whole exercise.

2 Gently twist your head and upper body to the right and place your right arm over the back of the chair. Keep turning your head until you are looking over your shoulder, and hold this position for five seconds.

3 Slowly turn to the opposite direction, removing your right arm from behind the chair and placing your left arm over the chair back. Turn your head to look over your left shoulder, and hold the position for five seconds.

4 Repeat steps 1 to 3 three times.

BACK RELAXER

It is a good idea to take a short break from sitting and working from time to time, by standing up or walking around. This is a good tension-reliever to do when you have a break.

1 Stand straight with your back against a wall. and raise your right knee up toward your chest, clasping the leg firmly with both hands.

2 Pull your knee close in to your chest, feeling the stretch in your back and shoulders, and hold for five seconds.

3 Gently release your leg, stand straight, and then perform steps 1 and 2 with your left leg.

4 Repeat steps 1 to 3 three times.

> If you feel as though you might lose your balance when doing this exercise, make sure you have something nearby to hold on to, such as a sturdy chair.

LEG RELAXER

These movements relax your legs and knees, which can get stiff or cramped if you have been sitting for a long period. Swinging your legs to and fro also gives you an almost childlike sense of freedom from stress.

1 Clear a space on your desk or table and sit on it so that your feet don't touch the floor.

2 Gently kick your legs back and forth, allowing them to swing freely.

3 Feel your legs gently loosening, and carry on swinging them for about 30 seconds.

FOOT RELAXER

Your feet and ankles can become stiff if you've been standing or even if you've been sitting in one position for a time. These movements will loosen and soothe tired joints.

1 Sit on a table or desk so that your feet don't touch the floor.

2 Rotate your feet at the ankle joints in a large circle. Continue for three complete circles as you feel your feet and ankles gently stretching.

3 Repeat step 2 in the opposite direction.

4 Repeat steps 2 and 3 three times.

HAND RELAXER

This exercise quickly releases tension in the hands and wrists that can easily build up when writing or working at a keyboard for any length of time. If you clear a space in front of you, you can do it at your desk while you are working.

1 With your palms facing downward, place your hands and forearms flat on the surface of the desk or table.

2 Slowly raise your fingers from the surface, still keeping your palms flat on the surface. Feel your fingers stretch, and hold for five seconds.

3 Keeping your fingers up, slowly raise your hands off the desk or table, keeping your forearms on the surface. Feel the stretch in your whole hand, and hold for five seconds.

RELAXATION TECHNIQUES

There are many different techniques you can use to relieve or reduce your reactions to stress, including changing your attitudes and changing the way you do things, changing your activities, changing your relationships and changing yourself. Many of these lie outside the scope of this book, though I would say that dealing with problems slowly, realistically and one at a time is vital. Make learning to deal with stress a gradual process in which you slowly develop confidence rather than an obsession to make sweeping changes which itself leads to further stress. However there are a few simple techniques that can help deal with stress by making you relax.

What is relaxation?

Most people think that relaxation is taking a break from the daily routine and sitting in front of the television or putting their feet up on the sofa with a magazine for a few minutes. Relaxation is more than this. To relax is to rest, to release tension and to allow your mind and body to be refreshed—and all this may have to involve a conscious decision. Any external or internal intrusion on this state of peace is a stressor and so must be deliberately put to one side. Sleeping—a nap or even a whole night—does not necessarily mean relaxation. How often have you gone to sleep exhausted but woken still feeling tired and tense? Relaxation is a skill that may have to be carefully practiced in order for it to have an effect on our minds and bodies.

Learning to relax

It is important to recognize the connection and the interaction of the mind and the body. Progressive relaxation, visualization and communicating with your senses are all self-relaxation techniques that help bridge the gap between your mind and your body and which can be learned to help you relax.

It is vital to be in tune with your body and respond to its needs. An increase in muscle tension is often the first sign of stress taking an effect on us: muscular tension and mental tension go hand in hand, each affecting the other. Whatever the cause of the stress, learning to relax the body can lead to relaxation of the mind.

Progressive relaxation

Try the following simple but effective exercise in progressive relaxation. It draws on and echoes some of the individual exercises detailed previously in the book, but it is a general technique that you can use anywhere, at any time, and in almost any circumstance.

Make yourself as comfortable as possible and take a few deep, regular breaths. Really settle yourself and fidget as much as you want before you start the exercise. Now focus your awareness on your breathing to prevent any outside thoughts or impulses distracting you. Then, starting from the top of your body and slowly moving down, tense and release each part of your body, holding the tension for a few seconds before releasing and being aware of the contrast. Feel the tension leaving your body as you relax. Systematically move down your body, working on each individual area in the following sequence: eyebrows; eyelids; cheeks; jaw; neck; shoulders; arms; hands; chest; abdomen; pelvis; buttocks; thighs; calves; feet; toes.

The basic principle is that if you are to learn to relax your body you must first be able to recognize when it is tense, and the difference between tension and relaxation. Letting go after tensing a muscle has a pleasant effect on the physical level and a more profound effect on the emotional level. It teaches that letting go and relaxing is not such a difficult task. It is accessible to you and it puts you back in touch with your body and gives you control over your feelings.

Communicating with your senses

With the various stressful demands of day-to-day life, many of us seem to run almost "on autopilot." We don't have the time to react to our senses, to stop and look, touch, taste, smell and feel the world around us. Communicating with our senses is an important relaxation technique, and this exercise will make you aware of your senses and help get your mind back in touch with your body. You will need a piece of fruit that you like for this exercise.

1 Find a place out in the open where you can sit comfortably and relatively undisturbed, for example a park or garden or even a balcony. Close your eyes and breathe calmly and evenly.

2 Keep your eyes closed and concentrate on your sense of hearing. Listen closely to all the sounds around you for at least five minutes.

3 Keeping your eyes closed, concentrate on your sense of smell for five minutes. Try and discern the various aromas around you. Bring the fruit to your nose and smell it.

4 Open your eyes and look closely at everything that surrounds you, appreciating the varied colors and shapes. Look carefully at your piece of fruit.

5 Slowly eat your piece of fruit. Savor the taste and chew each mouthful at least 15 times before swallowing it.

6 Now touch the things that are close at hand. Feel the various textures, weights, and shapes.

7 Try to spend at least five minutes on each sense. Remain sitting peacefully for a little while as you let yourself appreciate your environment in a truly sensuous way.

VISUALIZATION

With practice, you can actively picture or imagine yourself getting rid of tension, banishing negative stressful thoughts, becoming relaxed, and as you visualize this in a positive way it will actually happen.

1 Lie on your back on a firm but comfortable surface, with cushions or pillows supporting your head and under your knees keeping your legs slightly bent. Place your hands lightly on your abdomen and close your eyes, keeping them closed throughout the whole exercise.

2 Become aware of your breathing, keeping it slow, even and regular. As you breathe in, imagine the fresh, strengthening air being drawn into your lungs. On your outbreath, picture all the stress and tension slowly leaving your body as you breathe out.

3 Try to quiet all the background thoughts in your mind that act like distracting chatter. Calmly picture the space between your eyes and say the word "r-e-l-a-x" slowly and repeatedly in your mind. Feel the tension evaporating from that area.

4 Move your thoughts to your eyelids, eyebrows and all the muscles around your eyes and visualize them releasing tension as your mind continues to tell them to relax.

5 Make your way down your whole body to the tips of your toes, picturing every part releasing tension. Lie completely still for a minute or two.

6 Now starting from your toes, imagine positive energy flooding in and spreading slowly through your body right up to the space between your eyes, invigorating and revitalizing.

> If you find it difficult to get to sleep, try doing steps 1 to 5.

BREATHING

A vital aspect of relaxation is the awareness and control of breathing. The fact that we can't help but breathe, automatically, does not mean that we automatically breathe in the best way, the way that benefits us both physically and mentally. You can easily become accustomed to shallow breathing, rapid breathing, mouth breathing, or upper chest breathing. These methods will keep you alive but won't improve the quality of your life—indeed they may well be detrimental to it.

Stressful breathing stress is rapid and shallow, coming mainly from the upper chest. This adds to the stress on our bodies, because the muscles of the chest, shoulders, and neck become over-used and tense. Shallow breathing does not use the lungs to the full so we breathe even more rapidly in order to get enough oxygen; and carbon dioxide is not expelled efficiently. This increases the sensation of stress and leaves us physically and emotionally drained, irritable, and lethargic.

When we are breathing well, we rely on the diaphragm, the muscular membrane between the abdomen and lower chest, to do the bulk of the work. Diaphragmatic breathing is deeper and slower, and uses the lungs more fully. We breathe in the right amount of oxygen and expel carbon dioxide efficiently, leaving us refreshed and alert, and reducing tension in the chest, shoulders, and neck. The interaction between breathing and stress shows how intimately related are the mind and the body and how to relieve the *physical* effects of stress by a *mental* decision to alter our breathing.

The signs of being under stress or in a state of emotional harmony and calm are reflected in the way you breathe. Knowing this gives you control in shaping the energy of your emotions. You can reverse the build-up of stress and directly control your reactions and habitual responses to stressful situations by altering your breathing pattern.

To recognize the link between breathing and relaxation try the following exercise. You can do this sitting or lying down. Tighten up all your muscles so that your whole body goes tense. Hold them clenched tight for ten seconds and then relax and let go. Notice that as you were clenching your muscles, you were also holding on to your breath, and as you let go of the tension you also released your breath. This is a useful indicator of how you breathe under stress, but more importantly it shows the link between the outbreath and the release of tension. So as well as breathing in, we can learn to breathe out correctly and in so doing breathe away stress.

To assess which area you use to breathe, lie on your back, placing one hand on your abdomen, the other on your chest. Which area rises at the start of each breath? It should be your abdomen.

The following exercises will help you control your breathing and breathe in the best way. When doing them, ensure that you are not holding on to your breaths, and if you feel dizzy or faint at any point, stop immediately. Anyone with pulmonary of cardio-vascular problems should consult their GP before starting these exercises.

DIAPHRAGMATIC BREATHING

By focusing on your abdomen, this exercise helps you become aware of how you should feel when your diaphragm is powering your breathing. In time this conscious awareness will become unconscious and natural, but you can always return to this exercise any time you feel that stress is controlling your breathing.

1 Lie comfortably on your back with your legs on a low stool or a pile of cushions so that your legs are bent roughly at right angles at the knees.

2 Place your hands on your abdomen and breathe in slowly but deeply through your nose. Keep your shoulders and chest relaxed and feel your abdomen rising under your hands.

3 Slowly breathe out through your mouth and as you do so tighten your abdominal muscles and press them with your hands to feel the air empty out of your lungs completely.

4 Repeat steps 2 and 3 three times.

BREATH CONTROL

This exercise focuses on breathing in and breathing out as deliberate actions, rather than unconscious processes, so that you become aware that you can bring them under your conscious control in times of stress.

1 Lie comfortably on your back with your knees slightly bent so that your feet are flat on the floor. Your arms should be resting by your sides, your hands on the floor at your hips.

2 Concentrate on breathing in as hard as possible, through your nose, but simply relax in order to let the breath out through your mouth. Do this three times.

3 Lie relaxed and let your breath flow in but then concentrate on breathing out as hard as possible. Do this three times.

4 Now breathe in as hard as possible and breathe out as hard as possible, three times.

5 Relax and breathe in and out normally and gently for a further ten breaths, but make a conscious effort to notice each in-breath and each out-breath.

CLEANSING BREATHING

Feel the clearing effect as you slowly flush your sinuses with deep cleansing breaths that leave you refreshed and relaxed. Co-ordinating the switching between nostrils may be awkward at first, but just try to concentrate on feeling your breaths flowing in and out.

1 Sit comfortably, making sure that your head, neck, and trunk are upright. Keeping your mouth closed, breathe slowly and deeply in and out through your nose five times. Make sure you are breathing diaphragmatically.

2 Raise one hand and allow your thumb and index finger to rest on your face either side of your nose, ready to block each nostril as appropriate during the rest of the exercise.

3 Block off your right nostril and breathe in through your left. As soon as you have taken the breath in through your left nostril, block it off, releasing your right nostril at the same moment to allow your breath out of the light. Repeat this three times, breathing in through the left nostril and out though the right.

4 As soon as the last breath is expelled from the right nostril, keep the left blocked and take a deep breath in through the right. Immediately block the right nostril, releasing the left and breathe out. Repeat this three times, breathing in through the right nostril and out through the left.

5 Move your hand away from your face and take a further three breaths in and out through your nose.

Try to relax throughout this exercise and remember to breathe diaphragmatically.

MASSAGE

Massage is one of the best ways of reducing stress. There are techniques you can use by yourself as well as those performed with a partner and all have a potent effect on the release of tension, both physically and mentally.

During periods of stress the body tenses, as if to prepare itself for some form of physical action. If the physical action (which the body "expected") does not occur, the muscles will continue to feel tense and tight because they are "locked" in this preparatory phase. This in turn leads to feelings of tiredness and irritability and general aches and pains. Massage is excellent for directly relaxing the muscles, but it also has many other more general benefits that contribute to overall health: it boosts circulation and lowers blood pressure, assists digestion, helps the lymphatic system to dispose of toxins from areas of tension, and stimulates the release of endorphins—natural chemicals that the body produces to combat pain and enhance feelings of well-being. These physical effects coupled with the psychological benefits, if you are being massaged by a partner, of being touched and cared for by someone else combine to produce a powerful system of stress release with long-lasting results.

Massage can also be very satisfying for the masseur—both enjoyable to do and gratifying to see your partner's tension flow away. Even if you are inexperienced in massage you will soon gain confidence and the massage sessions will be successful if you remember a few points. Most of these points apply to self-massage as well as massage with a partner. Ensure that the room is warm enough, especially if your partner is going to remove clothing (note that many exercises, including the ones outlined here, can be done without removing clothes). Find comfortable positions, both for your partner and yourself. You should be relaxed, and both of you should be aware of your breathing, making sure that it is even and regular; your partner should take time to lie still and concentrate on his or her breathing both before and after the massage. Use the whole of your hand to massage, and do not press directly onto bones and joints as this is likely to be painful and will disrupt the soothing effect of your massage. Always start gently and keep your movements rhythmic. Perhaps most importantly, communicate with your partner: find out where the areas of tension are; make sure that the pressure you are applying is not too strong; ask him or her how it feels, which techniques and strokes they think are most effective; watch and listen carefully for their reactions.

Techniques

There are various types of massage that can be used for different results. In general, vigorous massage with quick, short strokes energizes and revitalizes, while smooth flowing strokes comfort and caress. As well as the exercises on the following pages, there are distinctive massage techniques that have technical names:

Effleurage is a long, flowing rhythmic stroke that is applied with an even pressure in one direction only. You use the whole of the hand to make contact with your partner. It is a good stroke with which to begin and end a massage session and has a gentle, calming effect.

Petrissage is a deeper technique that massages the body more firmly. Gripping with the whole hand, you roll and lift the muscles, holding them for five to ten seconds before releasing. It is an effective technique for large areas of tension such as the shoulders, back and legs where you can literally lift the tension away.

Wringing works both hands in opposite directions, grasping and rolling the muscles in a slow, rhythmic manner as if you were wringing out a cloth. This technique should be used only on fleshy areas of the body where the muscles can be grasped and rolled comfortably.

Percussion again uses both hands together in firm but not painful slapping, chopping, or cupping movements. You use the flat of your hand to slap; the edge of your hand to chop; and for cupping you use your slightly bent fingers and the edge of your palm near your wrist to form a cup shape that you bring down on the body with a rapid rhythmic movement. With all percussive techniques you should keep your wrists supple and be careful not to be too forceful.

Squeezing involves spreading your thumb wide and using the whole of your hand to get a good hold on a muscle and then squeezing with gently increasing firmness for about 10 to 15 seconds before releasing and moving on to another area. Don't hold or squeeze too hard—this should not be painful in any way. It is a good method for tired shoulders and aching calves.

Trigger point massage is a good technique to use over small knotted areas of muscle. Place your fingertips over the area and, using small rapid actions, move your fingertips backward and forward to dissolve the knot. Trigger point is a massage for releasing specific areas from tension.

Cautions

There are some conditions in which massage is not advisable. The main instances are listed below, but if you have any queries, seek the advice of a qualified medical practitioner or doctor.

- In the first three months of pregnancy.
- On areas with broken or inflamed skin.
- On areas of swelling.
- On areas of injury or tissue damage, such as over freshly broken bones or recent operation scars.
- On areas with specific skin complaints, such as eczema, psoriasis, or dermatitis.
- Over varicose veins or broken blood vessels.
- If your partner is undergoing medical treatment or is suffering from a particular ailment.

TEMPLE SOOTHER

This is a good massage to use toward the end of a relaxation session. It gently soothes away tension that has built up during the day and helps iron out those worry lines on your forehead.

1 Lie down on your back on a comfortable surface with your head supported by a cushion. Take a few slow, deep breaths to relax.

Partner

1 Sit on the floor, with your legs crossed, just behind the cushion.

2 Place both thumb pads gently between your partner's eyebrows so that your thumbs are touching.

3 Slowly and softly move your thumbs outward along the line of the eyebrows toward the ears.

4 Maintain your touch along the brow line and stop just before you reach the ears. Repeat 3-5 times.

NECK STRETCHER

This technique will help to stretch out and relieve tension along the neck and base of the head. It's a wonderful way to end the day and helps relax you before going to bed.

1 Lie down on your back on a comfortable surface with your head supported by a cushion. Take a few slow, deep breaths to relax.

Partner

1 Sit on the floor, with your legs crossed, just behind the cushion.

2 Place your hands underneath your partner's neck and interlace your fingers together, gently supporting the neck. Cup your palms loosely on either side of the neck.

3 Softly pull your partner's neck toward you and maintain the pull for 10 seconds. Be sure to keep your back straight. Repeat 3 times with gaps of 30 seconds in-between.

> Be careful not to cup your hands too tightly around your partner's neck. The action of pulling back should be smooth and gradual with no sudden or strong movements.

ARM AND SHOULDER LOOSENER

Feel the tension flow away as the swinging movement travels along your arm and shoulder. You and your partner can vary the effects by changing the position of the standing partner or trying gentle circular shaking

1 Sit upright on a chair with your feet a shoulders' width apart and your hands resting on your lap.

Partner

1 Stand in front and slightly to one side of your partner. With your nearest hand, lift his or her nearest hand and hold it lightly in a handshake clasp.

2 Slowly and rhythmically, gently shake your partner's arm from side to side for about 30 seconds, and then shake it gently up and down for a further 30 seconds.

3 Repeat steps 1 and 2 on the other side.

NECK MASSAGE

This is most effective if the seated partner relaxes his or her head and neck so that the masseur can feel and move the full weight of the head.

1 Sit upright on a chair with your feet a shoulders' width apart and your hands resting on your lap.

Partner

1 Stand behind your partner and place one hand on his or her head or forehead, for support and reassurance. With your other hand, place the thumb on one side of the muscles at the back of the neck and the fingers on the other side.

2 Starting at the base of the neck, slowly and gently pinch your thumb and first two fingers together. Start with a light touch, gradually increasing the strength of the grip as you feel your partner relax.

3 With this same gentle gripping motion, move slowly all the way up the neck to the base of the skull and slowly down again. Continue for about five minutes.

This should be a gentle, not a painful, technique, a gradual release of tension in an area most people

ARM RELAXER

The arms tend to be in constant use, and tension here can easily be transmitted along to your shoulders, neck and head so it's important to keep the arms relaxed.

1 Sit comfortably with your hands facing upward, resting on your lap. Place your right thumb on the inside of your left forearm close to your wrist.

2 Gently but firmly press your thumb into the muscle on the inside of your arm and slowly move up toward your elbow, pressing all the time.

3 Turn the left arm over and place your right thumb on the other side of your forearm close to the wrist and again slowly move up toward your elbow as you press into the muscle.

4 Repeat steps 1 to 3 with your left thumb on your right arm.

SHOULDER RELAXER

Most people find that tension noticeably builds up in the shoulders, and this is a very effective way of releasing it. Start the massage with a light touch and then progress to a grip as firm as is comfortable.

1 Sit comfortably with your head facing forward and your arms relaxed by your sides.

2 Bring your left hand across and place it on your right shoulder, next to your neck. Hold your left elbow with your right hand for stability.

3 With your fingers at your back and your thumb in front, grip the muscle on top of your shoulder gently for ten seconds.

4 Slowly work your way along your shoulder, gripping each area for ten seconds at a time. Work back and forth for about a minute, and then relax, letting your arms drop.

5 Repeat steps 2 to 4 on the other side.

LOWER LEG LOOSENER

Tension easily develops in your lower legs, especially if you stand for long periods. This massage is good for loosening tight muscles.

1 Sit comfortably on the floor with your legs stretched straight out in front of you.

2 Draw one leg toward you so that your foot is flat on the ground. Place your hands on either side of your calf muscles so that your thumbs are touching at the back and your fingers touching at the front.

3 Starting at the top of your muscle just under your knee joint, gently press your thumbs into the calf muscle and, keeping the gentle pressure, slowly slide your hands down to your ankle. Repeat this movement three to five times.

4 Repeat steps 2 and 3 on your other leg.

FOOT RELAXER

Feet get tired, stiff and tense, especially by the end of the day. Massaging along the length of your feet gradually relieves this.

1 Sit comfortably on the floor with your legs stretched straight out in front of you.

2 Move your left leg and rest your left foot on your right thigh so that your legs form a figure 4.

3 Place your thumbs on your heel, one in front of the other on an imaginary line running along the middle of the sole of your foot.

4 Gently, firmly and steadily, slide your thumbs up in a line toward your toes. Then repeat this action either side of the imaginary central line so that you are stretching your instep and the outside edge of your foot as well. Continue for about a minute.

5 Repeat steps 2 to 4 with your right foot.

INVIGORATOR

Stress can make you feel tired and drained of energy. This simple technique has a wonderful tingling, revitalizing effect.

1 Sit comfortably and move both hands up so that your middle fingers are resting on the opening to your ears.

2 Slowly move your fingers up and around so that you are lightly tracing the outline of your ears, round and back and round again.

3 Keeping soft contact between your ears and fingers, gradually quicken the speed of your circling. Continue for about 30 seconds.

HAND REVITALIZER

Almost all the work we do involves the hands, and they can easily become strained, tired, and stiff with tension. This technique both relaxes and revitalizes and is an excellent one to end a massage session in which you've been using your hands. It is a good idea to do short versions of this massage throughout the day to stop tension developing in your hands.

1 Sit comfortably and place the thumb and index finger of your left hand on either side of the webbing between the thumb and index finger of your right.

2 Gently pinch the muscle between your thumb and finger and maintain the pressure for five seconds. Work your way around the muscle pinching, holding and releasing as you move, then do the same with the muscles between each finger of your right hand.

3 Repeat steps 1 and 2 with your right thumb and index finger massaging your left hand.

NUTRITION

One of the most important sources of energy that affects the quality of life is food. A deficient diet leads to low energy levels and a greater susceptibility to stress and its harmful effects on the body.

Our modern, stressful world is a time-oriented society, preoccupied with speed, efficiency and instant results—a fast world needing fast food. Food in its original, natural state tend to be "packaged" by nature with the nutrients the body needs to utilize that food. However, fast food is often processed food: food that has lost many of its nutrients in the manufacture and packaging process. The nutrients that the body needs to convert the food are not available with the food, as they would be in nature, and so the body has to draw on its own nutrient reserves to compensate. In addition, processed food tends to contain various synthetic or chemical additives to preserve, stabilize, color it, and so on. The body needs to break down and eliminate these artificial ingredients and uses up precious energy and nutrients in doing so. Diverting energy and nutrients in this way can slow down the whole process of digestion and affect your metabolism.

The more you consume food containing artificial additives and other foodstuffs such as alcohol, coffee, and tea, the more you subject your body to energy stressors. They are stressors because they create a lot of metabolic work without the necessary nutrients and contain ingredients that the body has to detoxify. During periods of stress, the body also uses its reserves of vitamins and minerals as it endeavors to preserve health and survive stressful responses. Without a nutritious, balanced diet the body will then constantly be behind in the losing battle for energy, leading to negative effects on health and well-being.

Energy and a healthy diet

In contrast, the positive reactions to choosing the right food for your body can make you feel fantastic. A healthy diet will supply you with a steady stream of energy, have a beneficial effect on your immune system, and build up resistance to stress.

Most of our energy comes from carbohydrates, of which sugar and starch are the main types. There are natural and refined sugars and starches, and of course it is the naturally occurring variety that are best—they contain the nutrients the body needs to help utilize the food. Natural sugars are found in fruit and vegetables and their pure juices, while refined sugars are found in canned and bottled drinks, biscuits, sweets, and cakes. Bread and pasta made from wholegrain or wholemeal flour, brown rice, pulses and wholegrain cereals are good sources of natural starch, while white flour, bread, pasta and rice contain refined starch.

Fats are an important, concentrated source of energy, but we often consume too much and consume fats of the wrong sort. We should eat, in moderation, unsaturated fats, such as olive oil, and food containing essential fatty acids, such as sunflower oil, oily fish, and fresh nuts and seeds; we should try to reduce our intake of saturated fat, such as that found in meat.

Protein is a good source of energy and is vital to the body as a basis for building. It is needed for repairing damaged tissue and maintaining a healthy immune system and is found in meat, fish, poultry, eggs, dairy and soya products.

The other main components of a healthy diet include the essential vitamins and minerals found in fresh vegetables and fruit and, of course, water—obviously essential for human life and vital in a number of ways for the efficient working of our bodies.

Eating to reduce stress

Trying to achieve a healthy balanced diet and following the guidelines below should make you feel better and help to relieve, and make you more resilient to stress.

- Try to choose food as close to its natural state as possible.
- Eat three meals a day, i.e. breakfast, lunch, and dinner.
- Eat five helpings of fresh fruit and vegetables every day.
- Drink eight glasses (or two litres) of water a day.
- Eat within regular intervals—don't allow your stomach to be empty for long periods.
- Choose lean cuts of meat or cut off excess fat before cooking.
- Don't binge on refined carbohydrates such as sweets, cookies, or cakes when you feel hungry.
- Try to substitute fruit, vegetables, or cereals when you find yourself craving sweets.
- Watch your intake of alcohol, tea, coffee, and soft drinks. Try to have as little as possible.
- Add less salt and sugar to flavor food.
- Try to enjoy your food in a relaxed, unhurried manner, and chew each mouthful thoroughly before you swallow.

INDEX